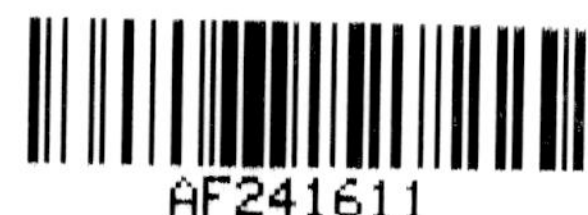
AF241611

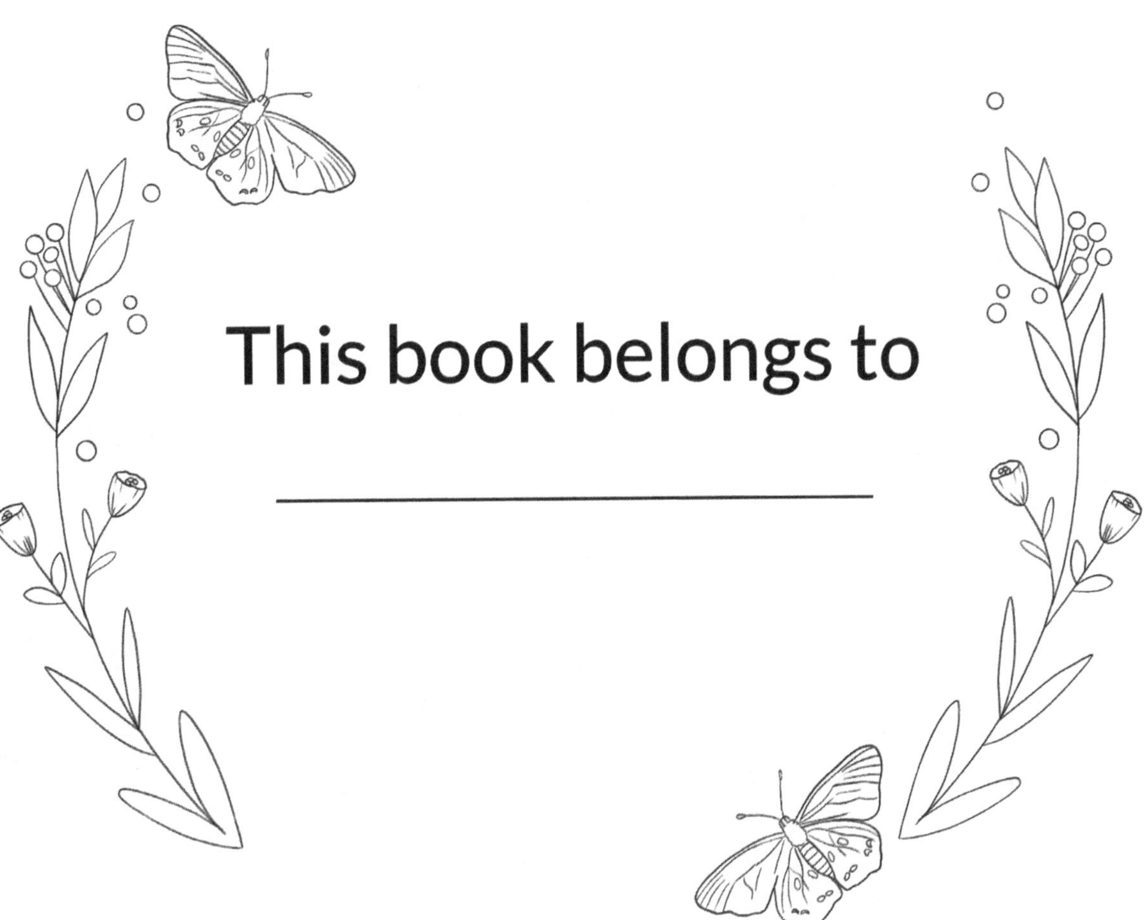

This book belongs to

____

Share your colorings on Instagram and
tag @dragonflyarts_coloring
#dragonflyarts_coloring

I'm sharing free pages for download on my Instagram

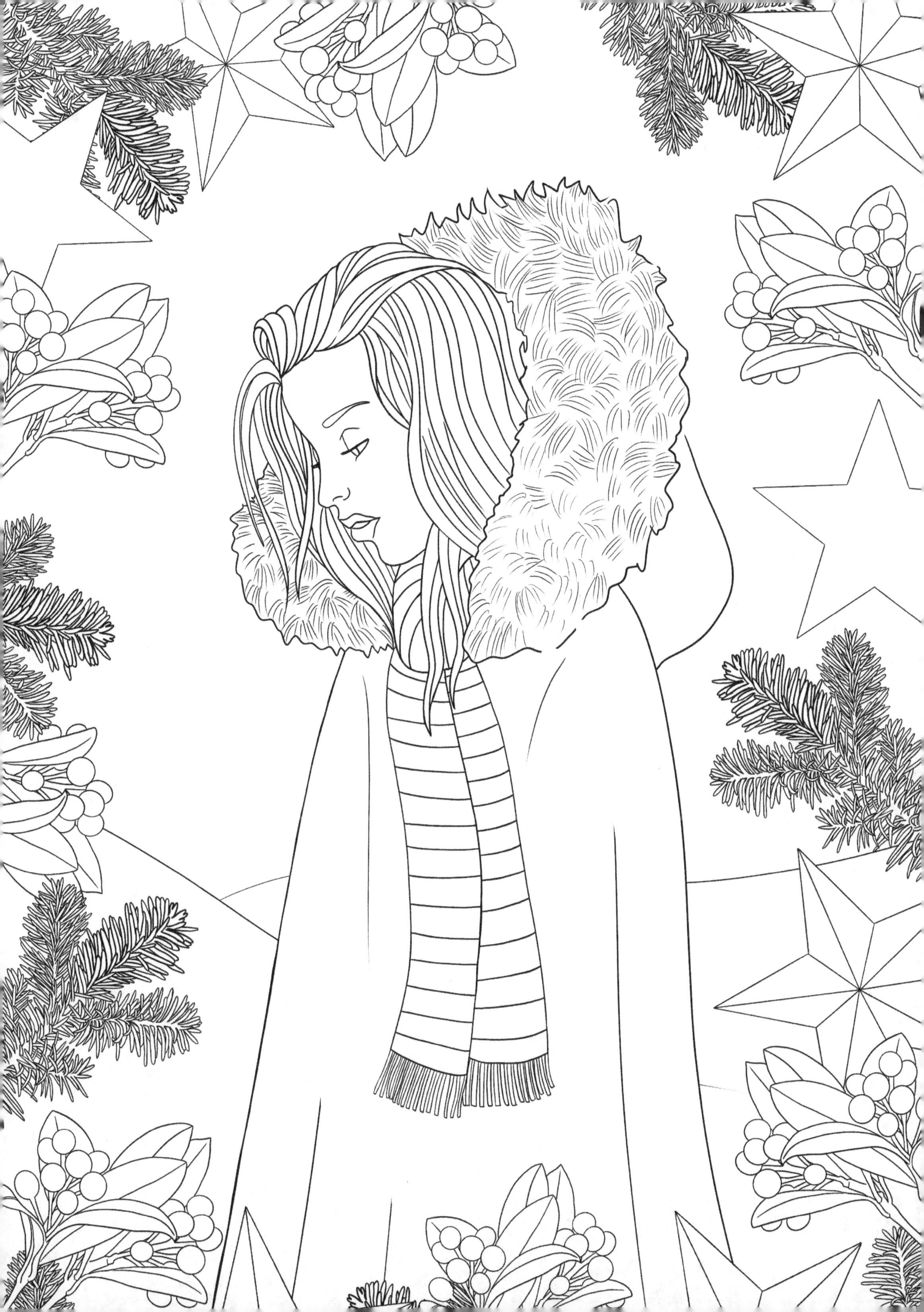

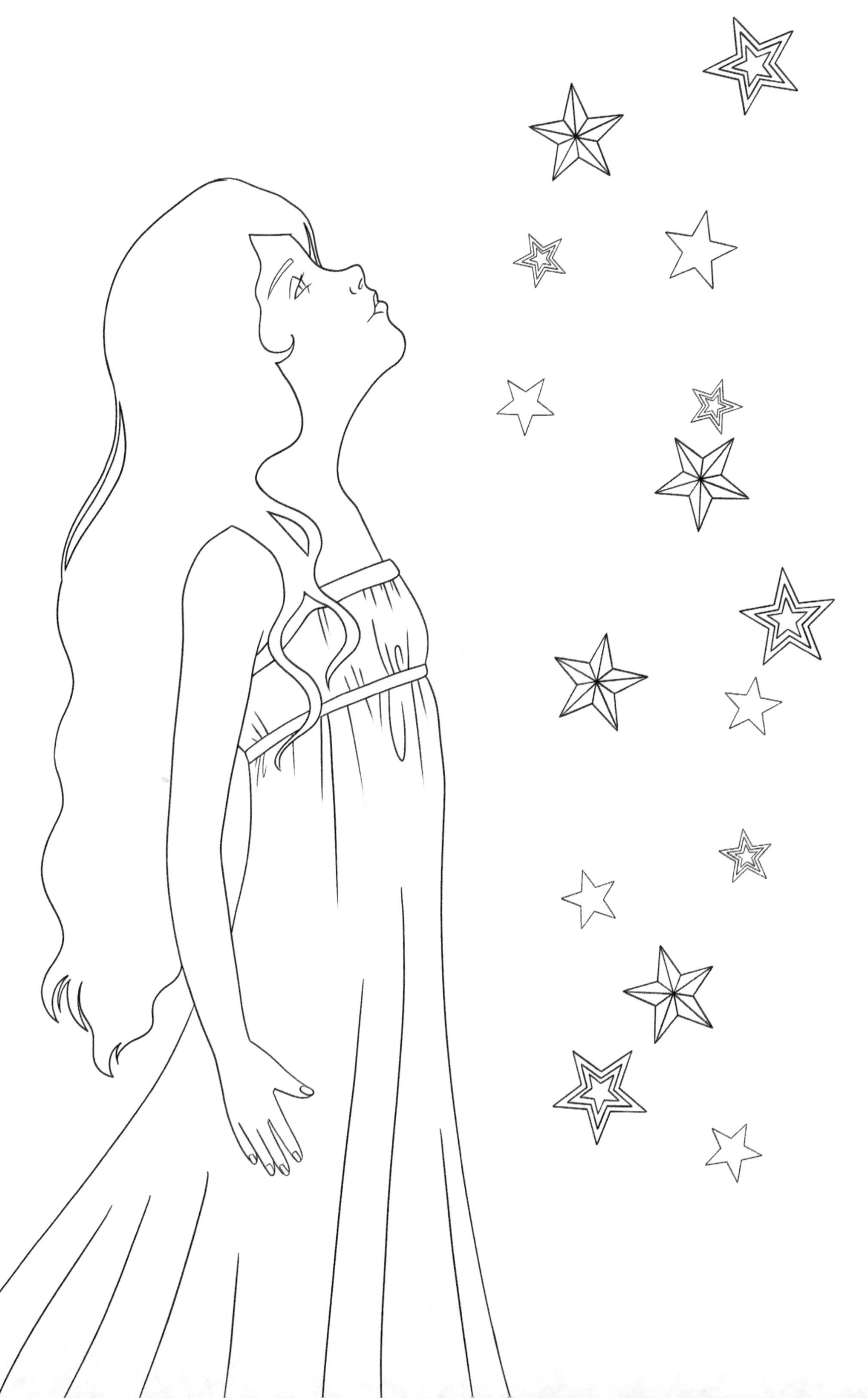

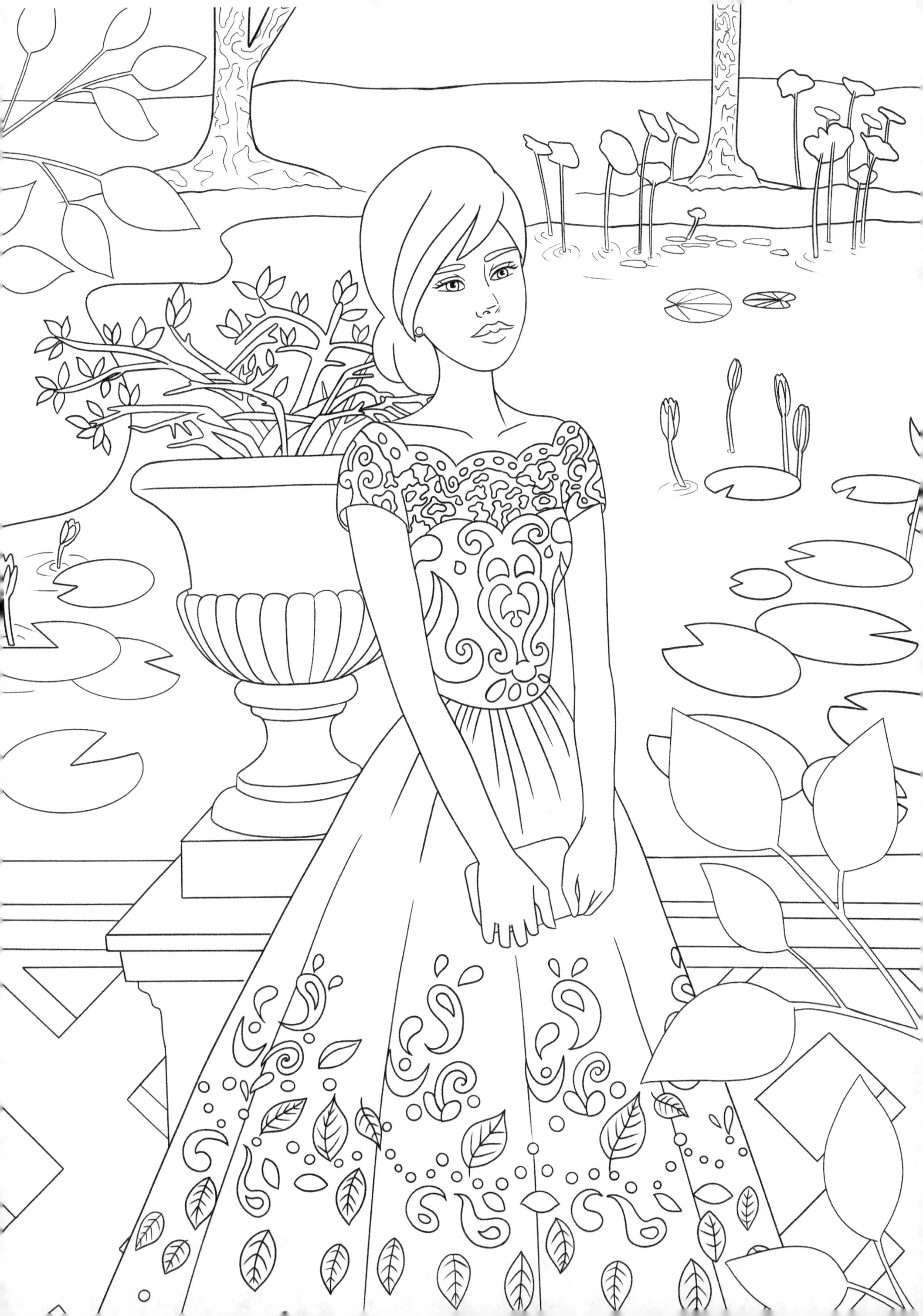

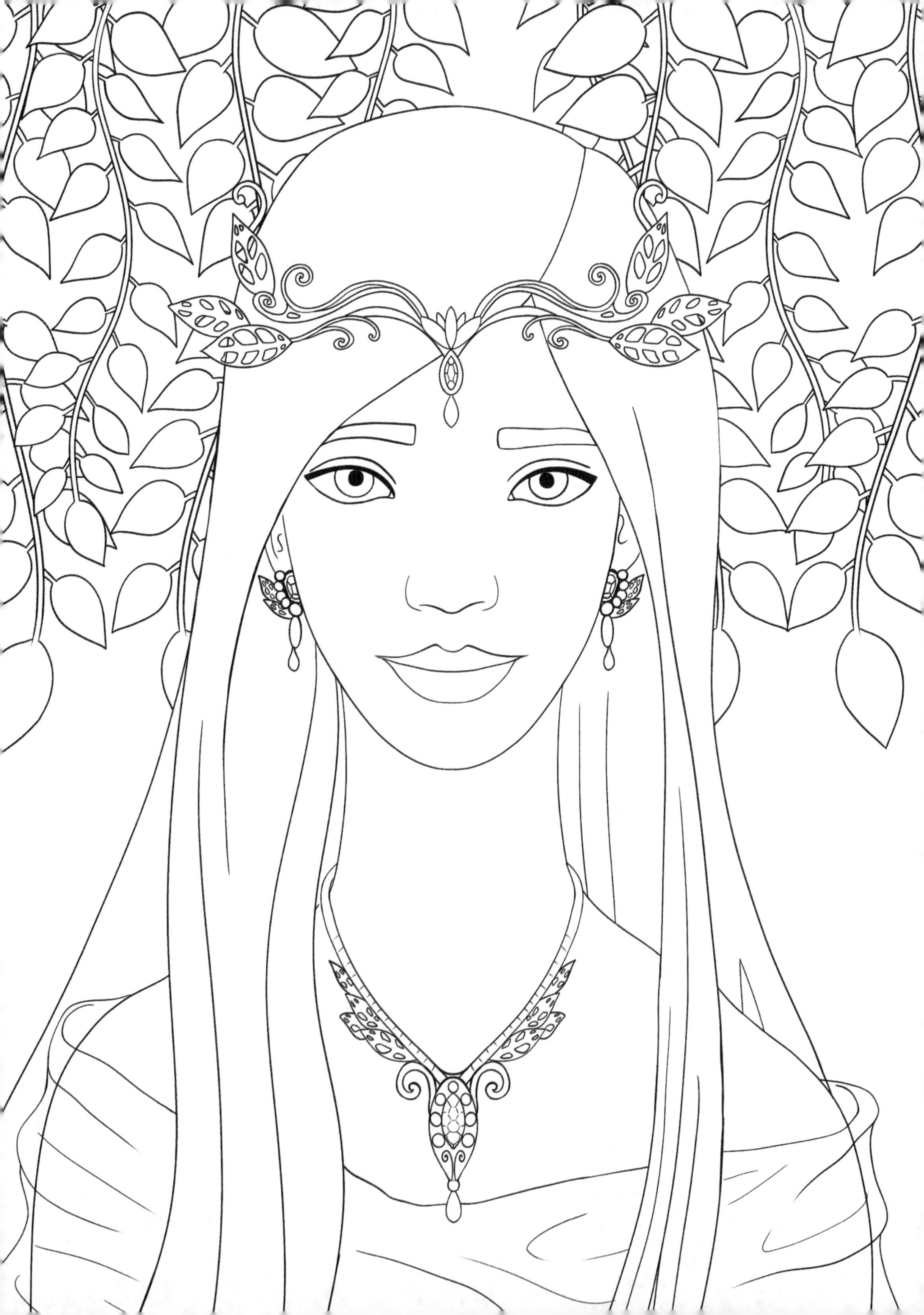

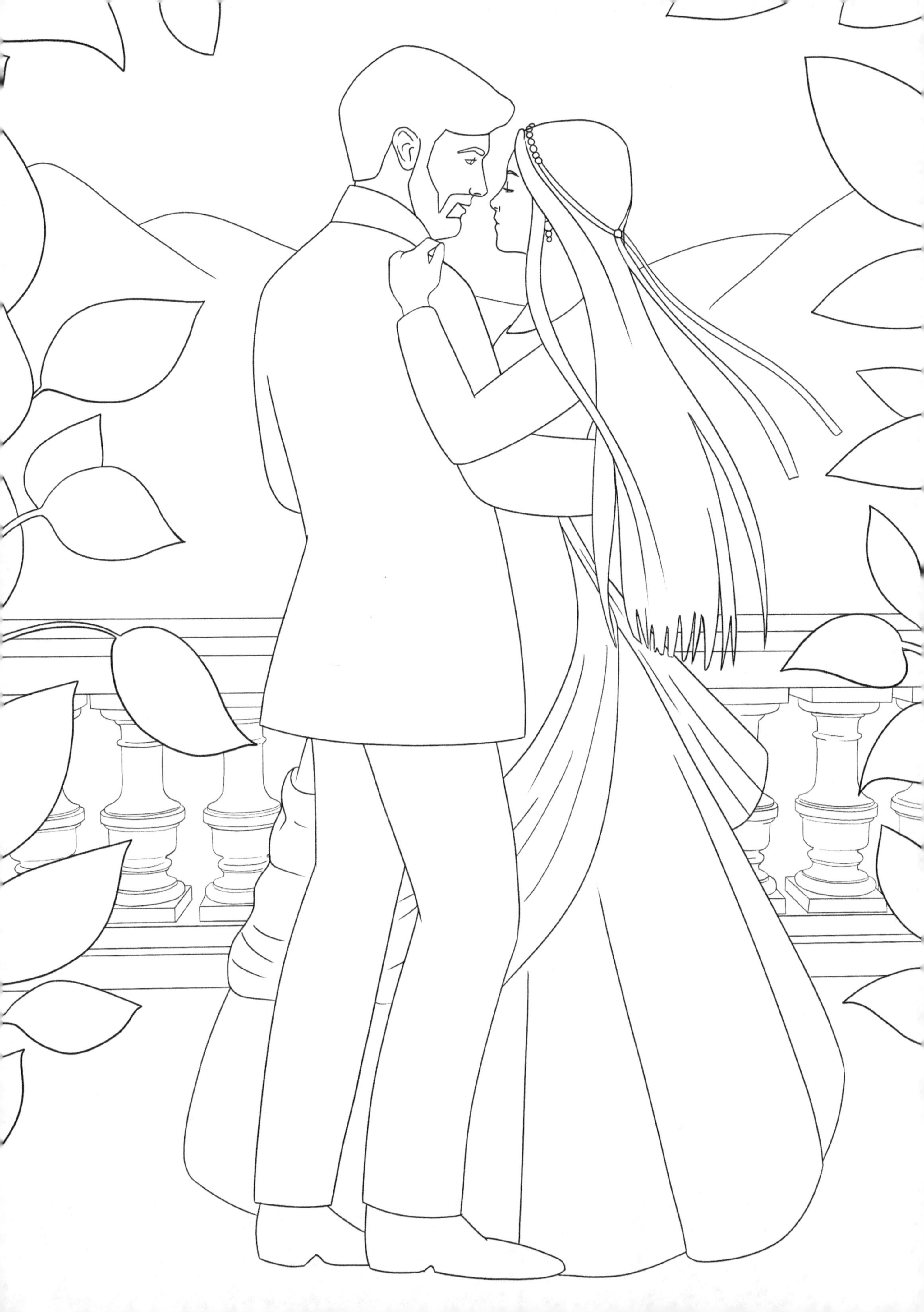

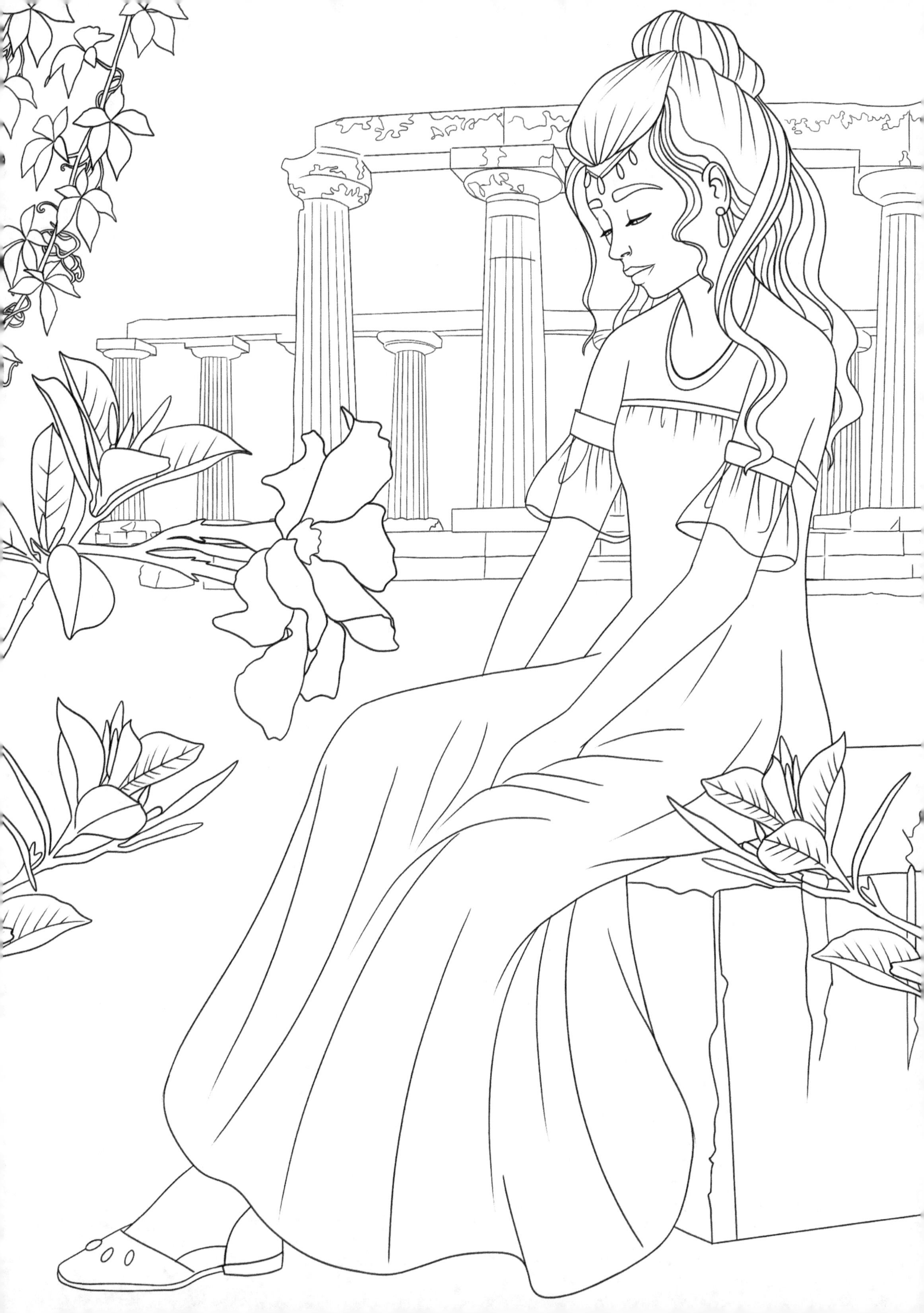

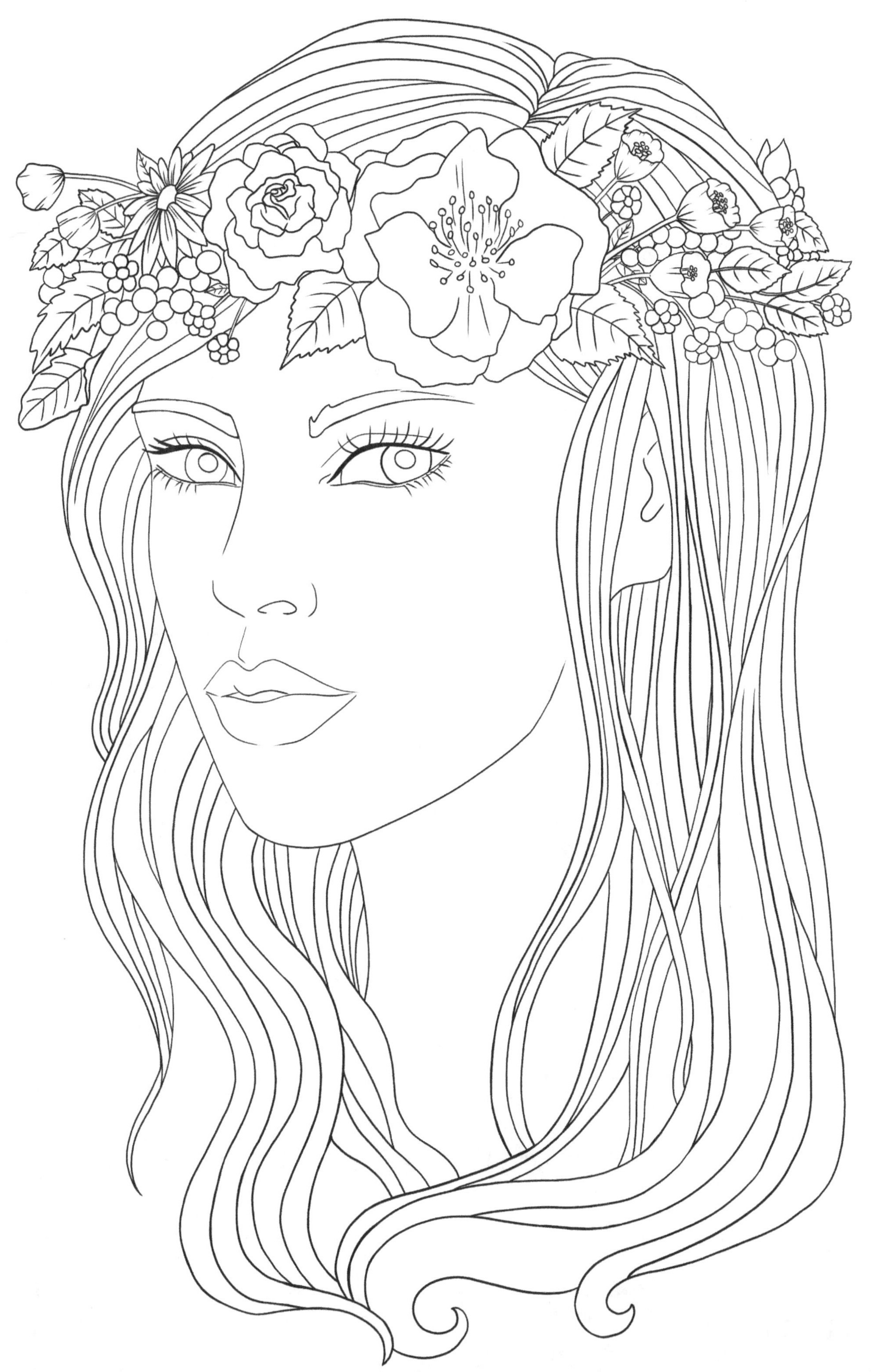

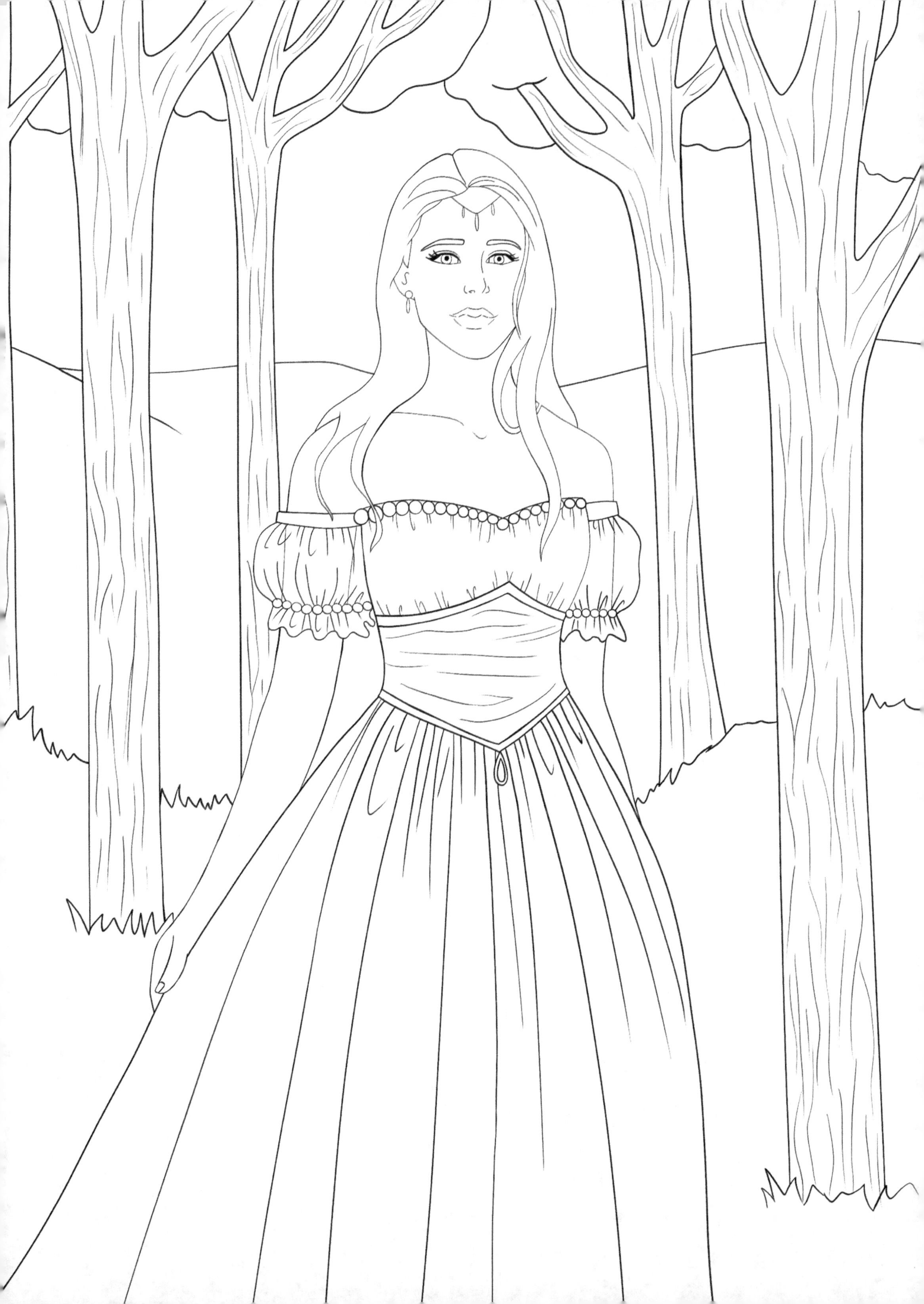

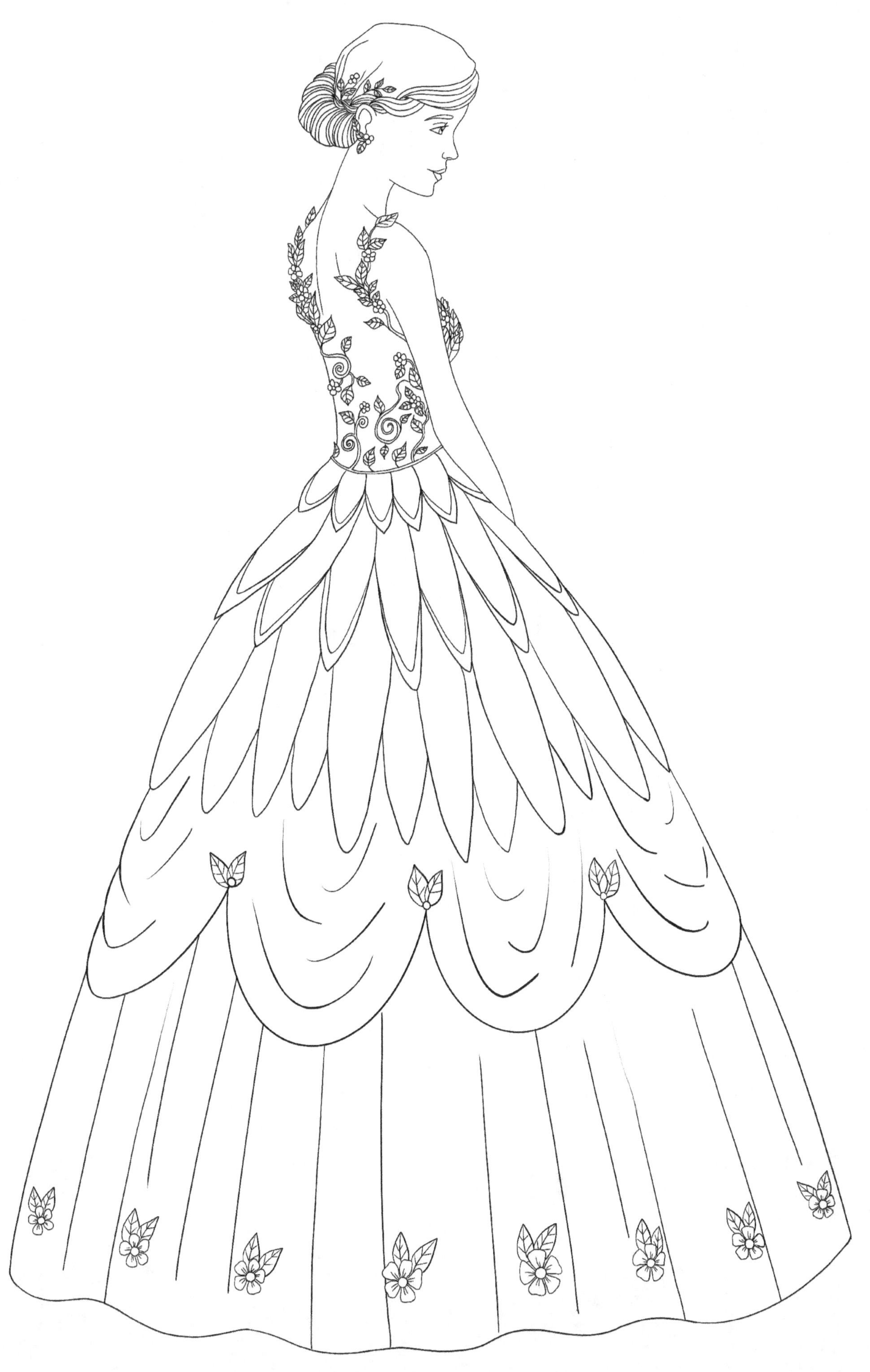

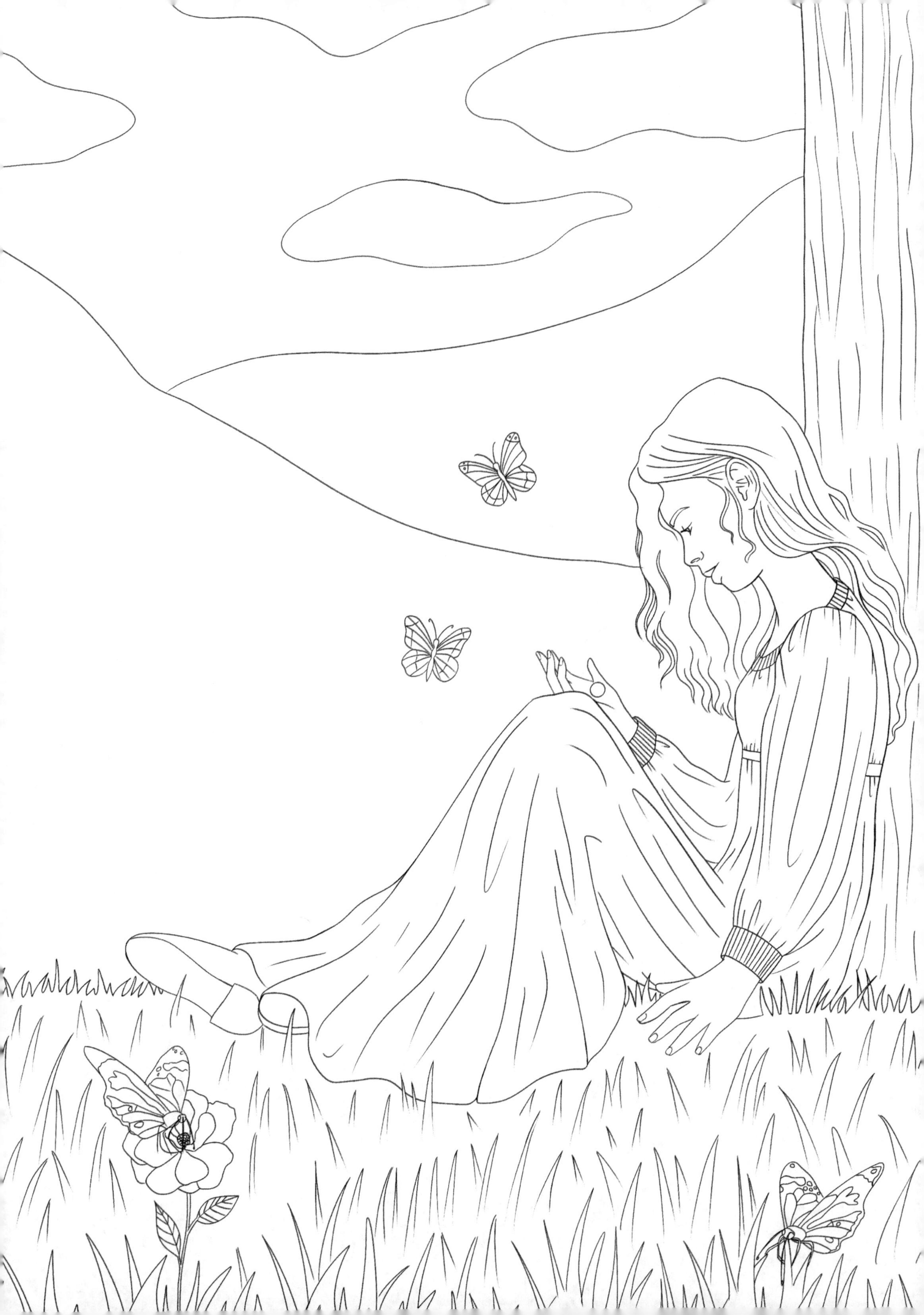

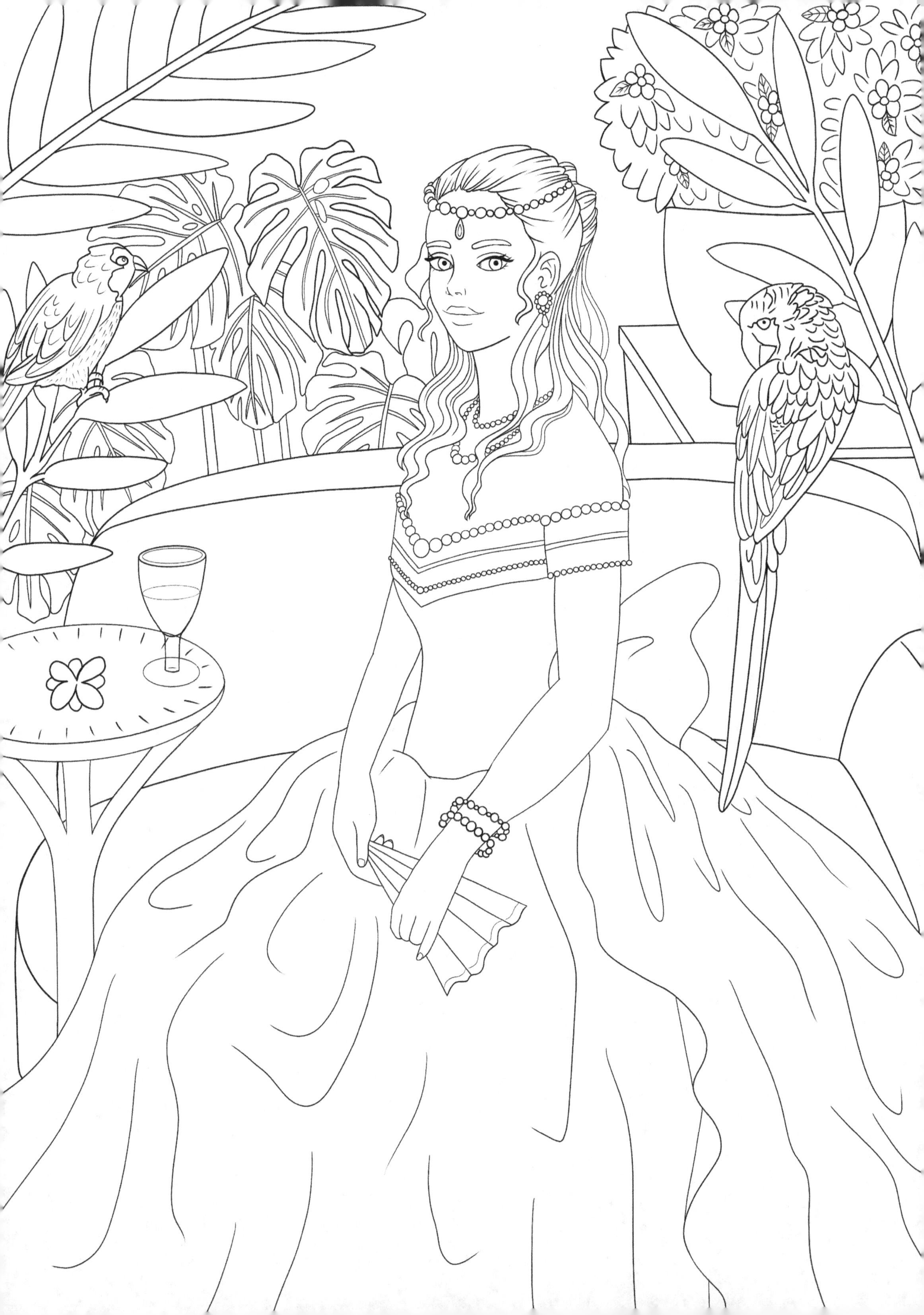

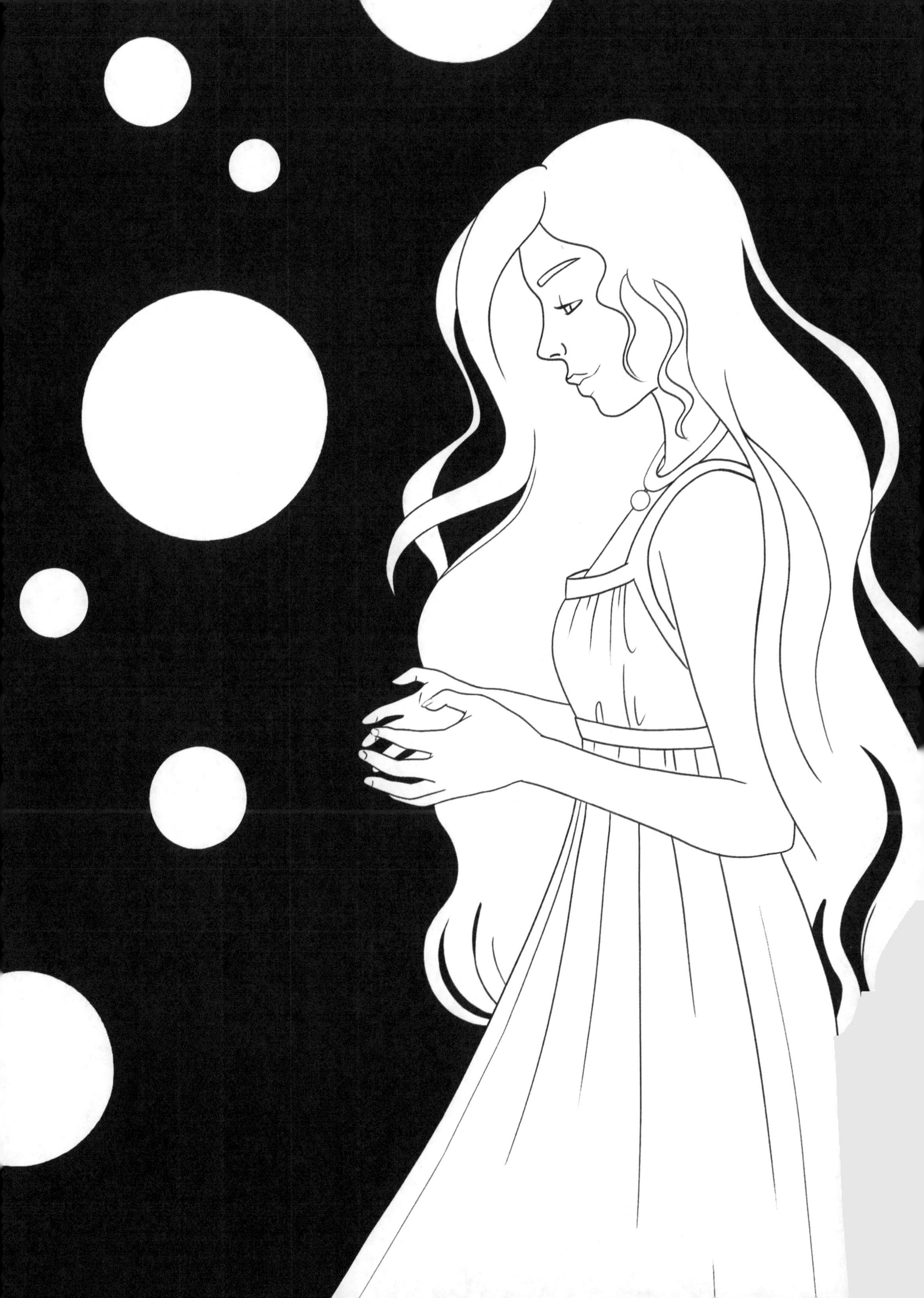

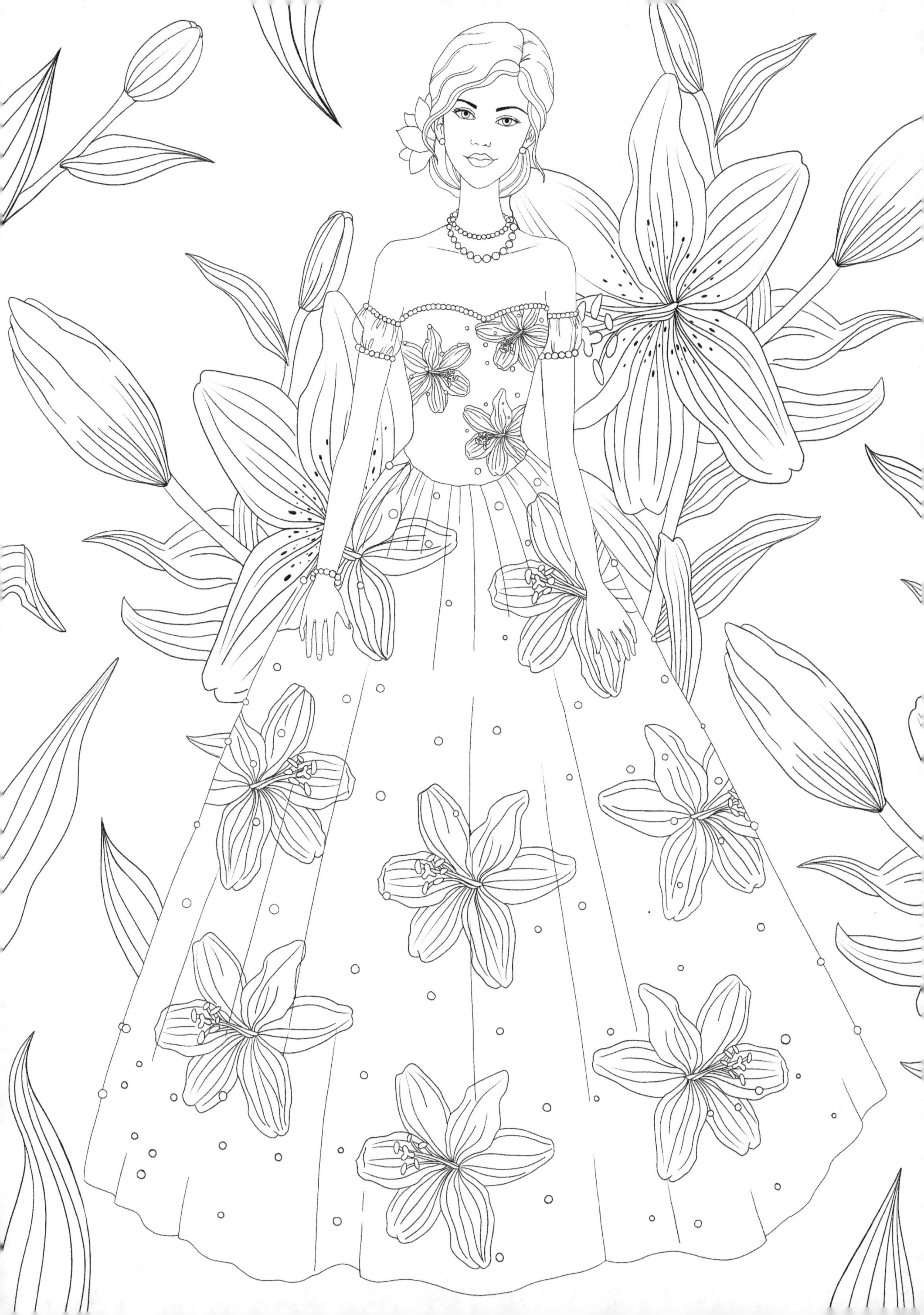

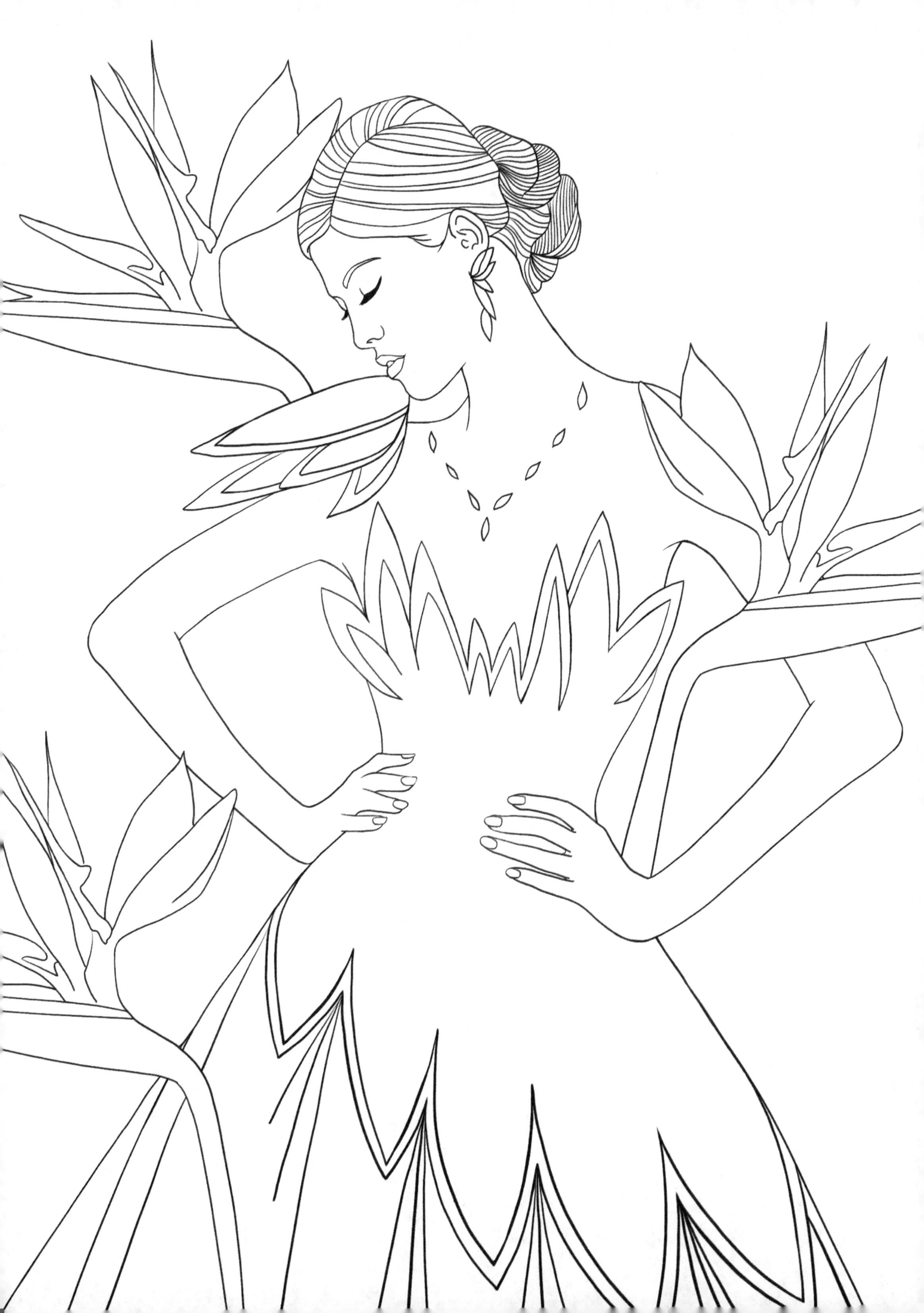

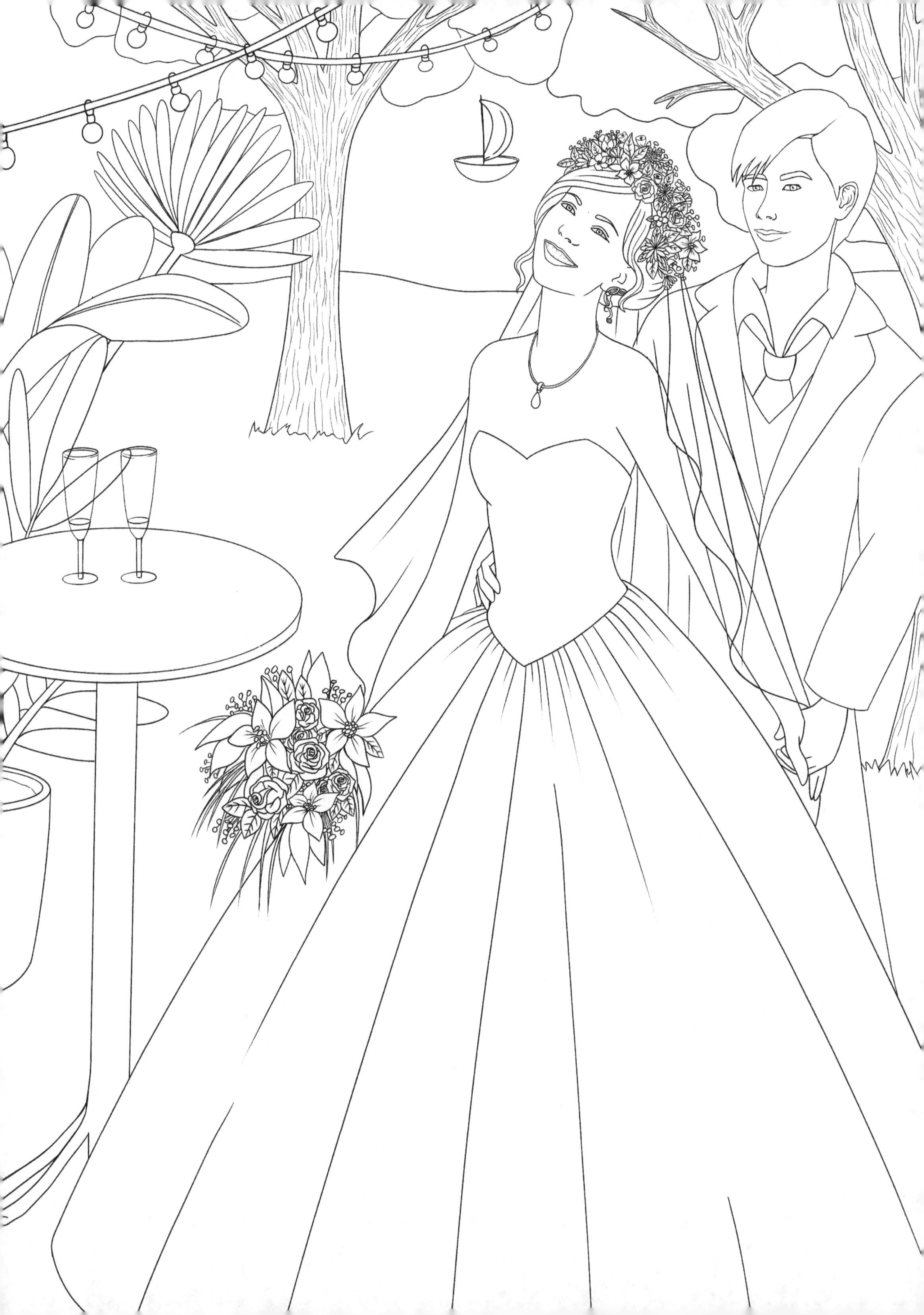

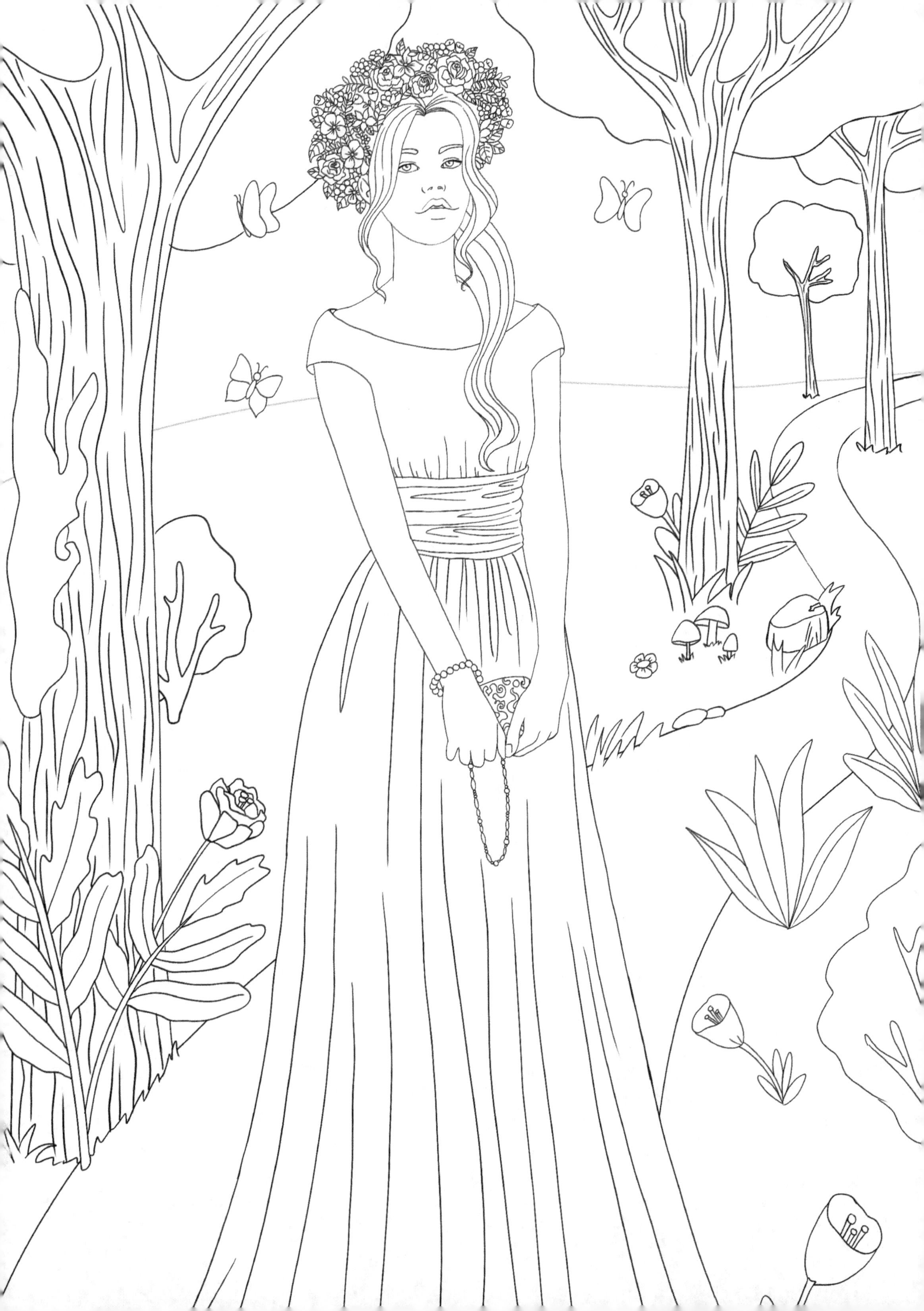

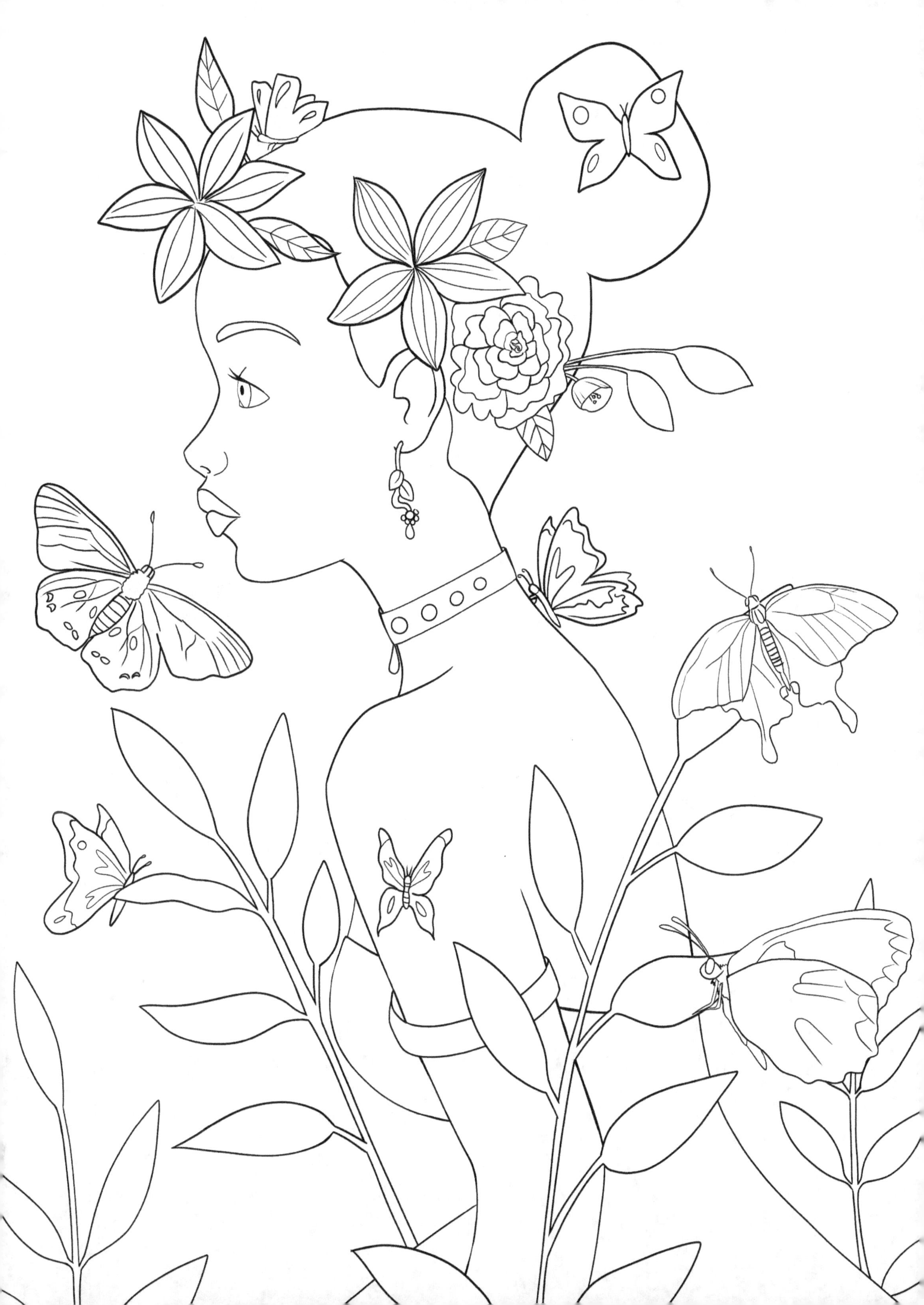

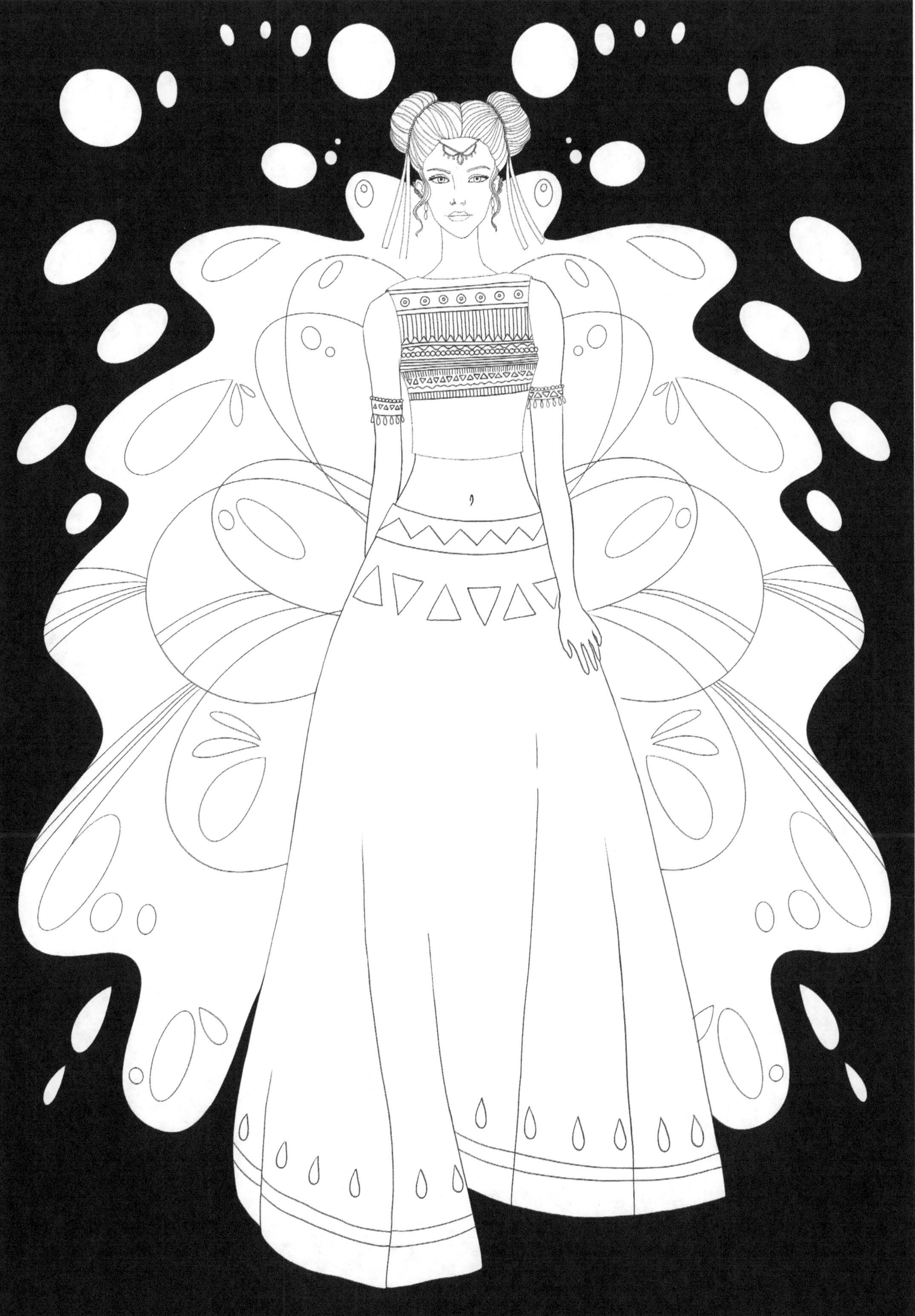

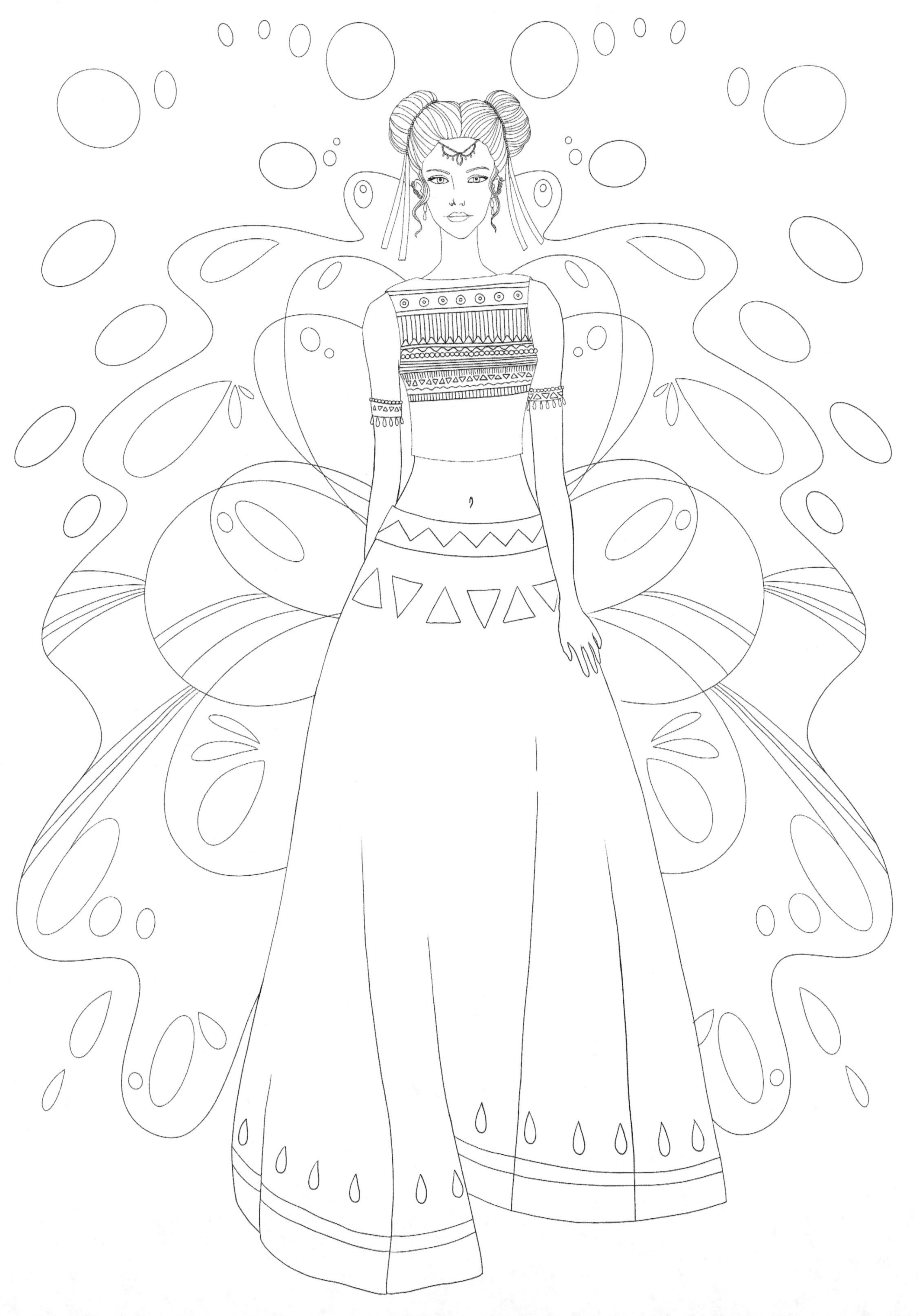

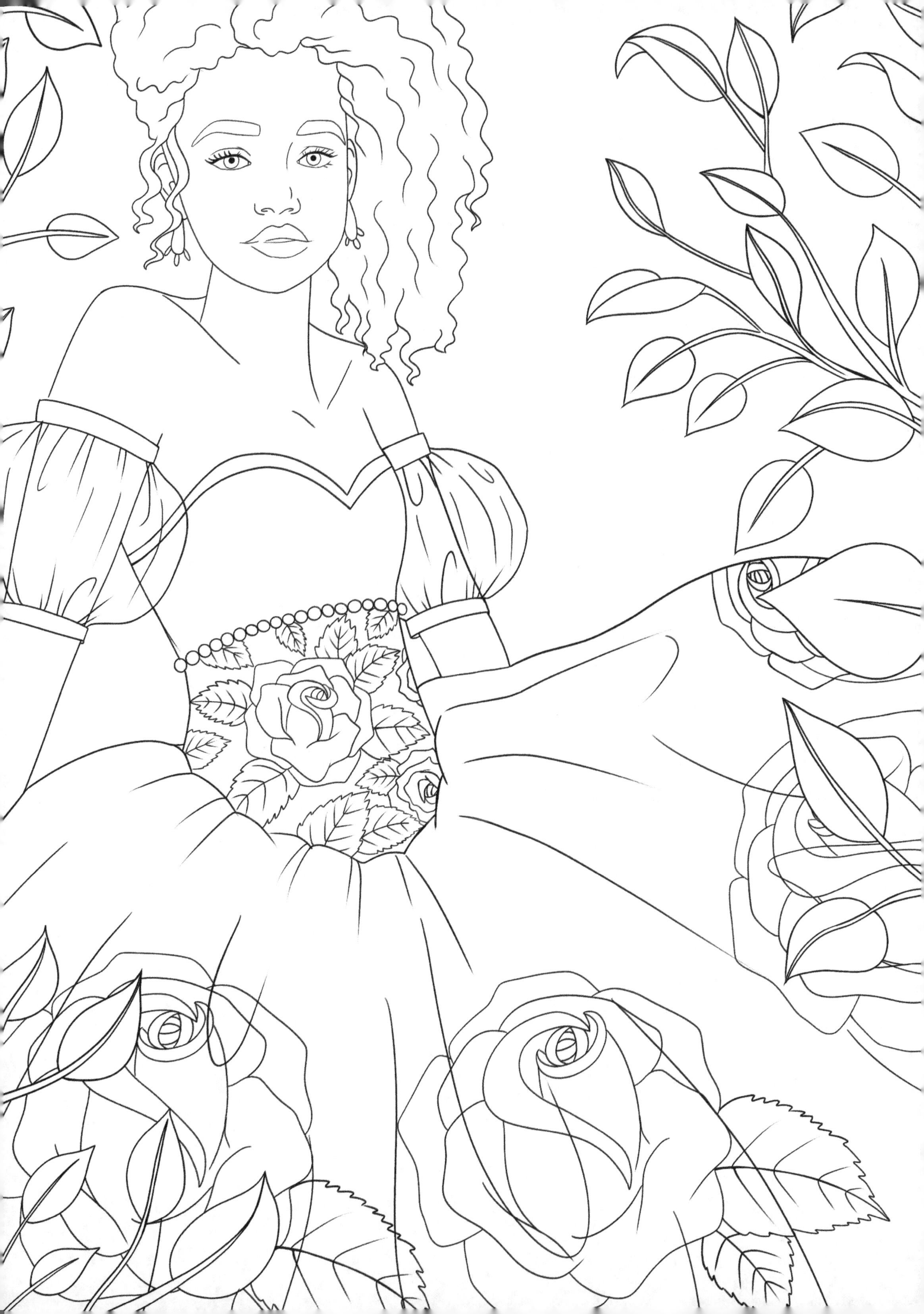

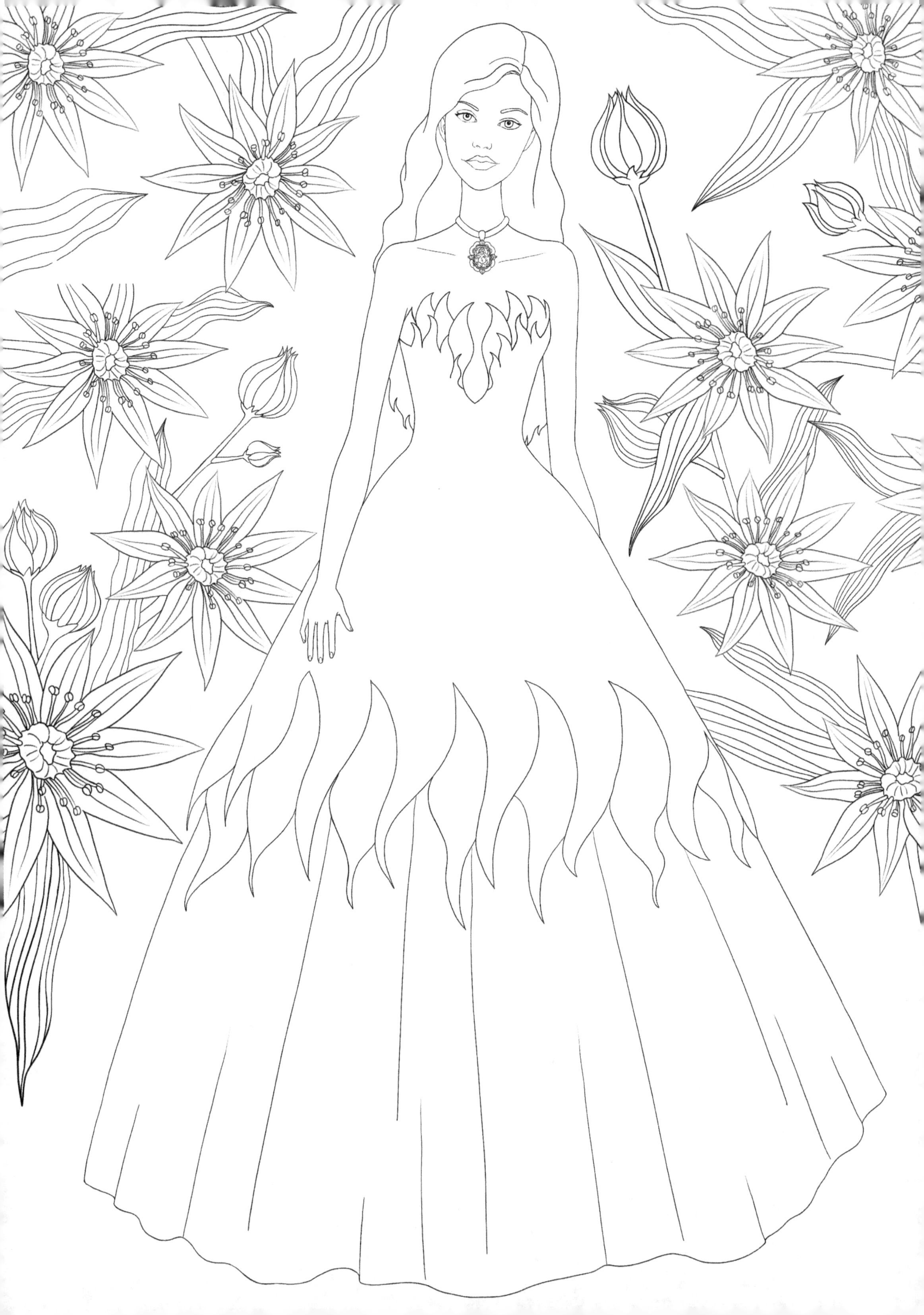

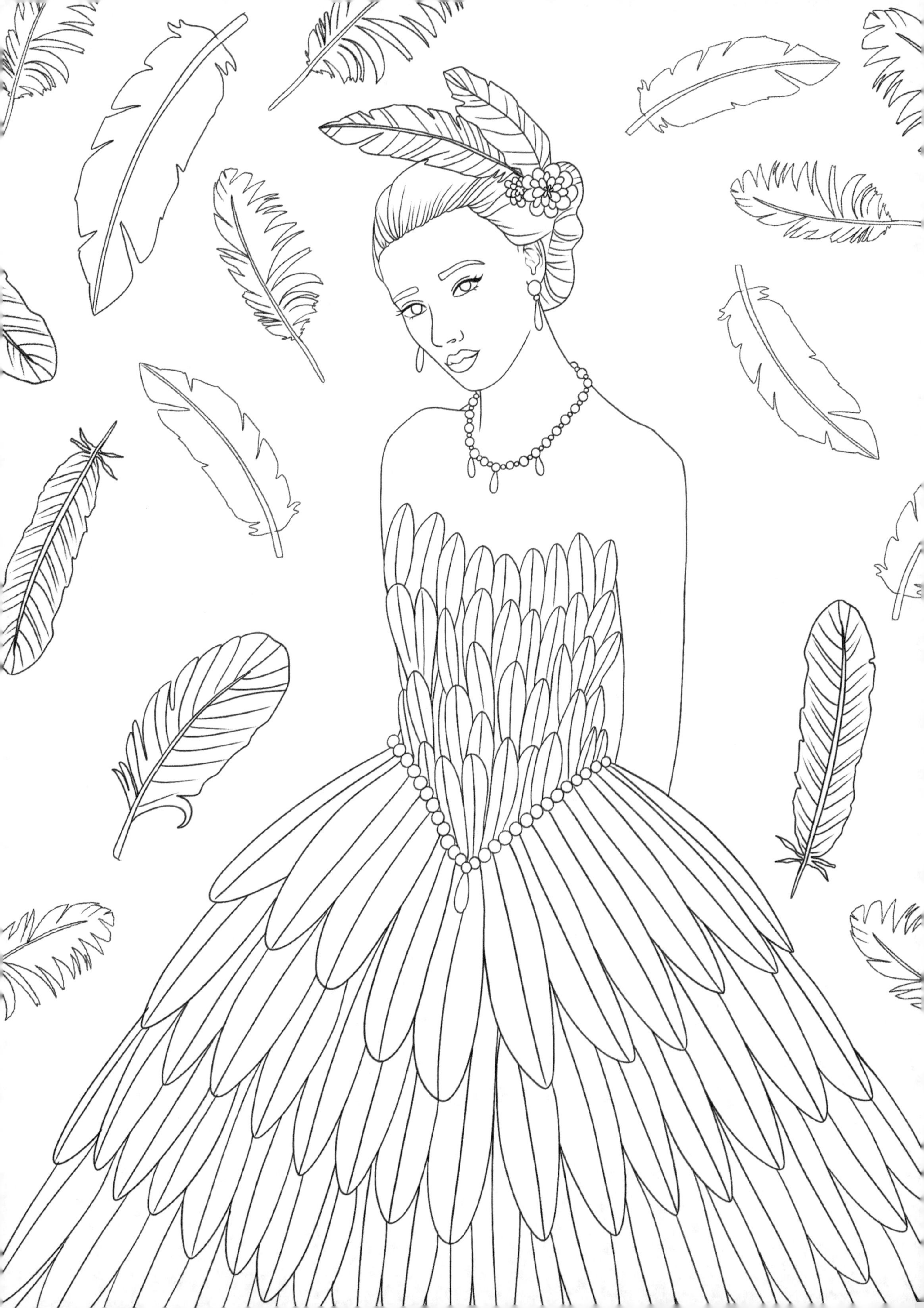

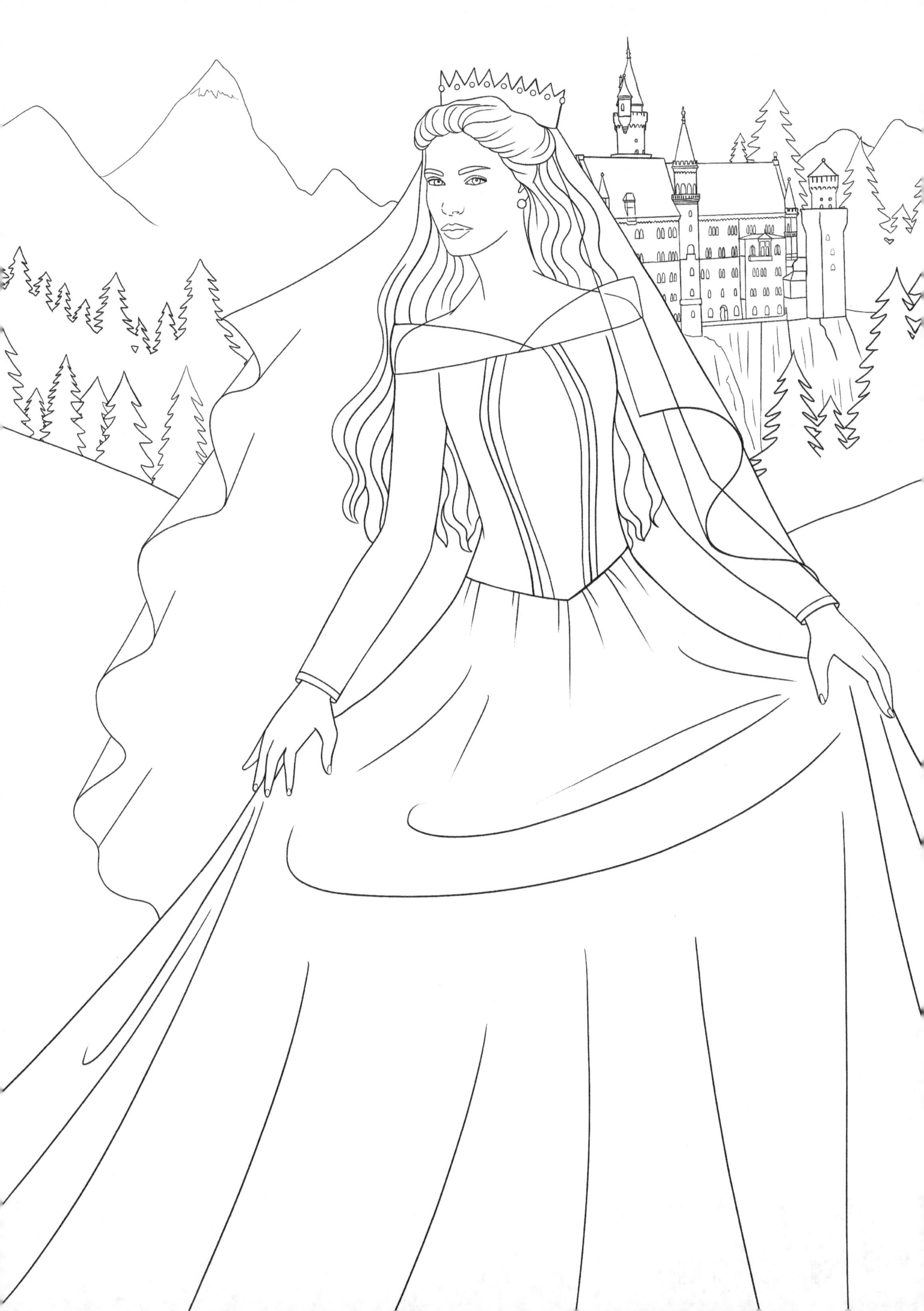